LOVE SONGS FOR BOYS

By the same author

Poetry

Ghostipus
The Book of Moons

Non-Fiction

The Parable of His-Story

LOVE SONGS FOR BOYS

Keone

Love Songs for Boys
by Keone

Published by La Pus Press 2022
copyright @Keone 2022

Keone has asserted their right under the Copyright, Designs and Patents Act 1988 to be identified as the author of this work

David's Song copyright David Nazario 2022

This book is sold subject to the condition that it shall not, by way of trade or otherwise, be lent, resold, hired out, or otherwise circulated without the publisher's prior consent in any form of binding or cover other than that in which it is published and without a similar condition
including this condition being imposed on the subsequent purchaser

First published in the United Kingdom in 2021
This edition published by La Pus Press, Wales in 2022

A CIP record for this book is available from the British Library

ISBN: 9781739947934

Scorching the Gorse was first published in Salopoet

Distractions was first published in Coasters

Swallows at Patmos was first published in Whisker II

Atlantis was first published in Sentinel

cover design and illustrations by Keone

for those who are both

Contents

Preface to the Second Edition	ix
David's Song	xii
Have You Got a Face Pic?	2
Boom Bang-a-Bang	3
Hair	4
Holy	6
Under Armour	7
The Rec	8
Atlantis	9
For the Ancestors	11
Swallows in Patmos	12
Flamenco	13
In Halls	14
The Emptied	15
Ghost Trees	16
The Once Bowl	17
Boy	18
Beautiful Stranger	19
Distractions	20
The Hunt	21
There You Go	22
Feral	23
Shelling	24
Husband of Water	25
Mermen	27
In the Pool	28
Green Man	29
Roots	30
The Consolation of Trees	31

Dancing with Oby	32
Scorching the Gorse	33
Samurai	35
Castle in Time	37
Ironing	39
Music Without Words	40
Major Arcana	41
Roses	43
The Nun Fish	44
Single Bed	46
Amusement	47
Alcyone	48
After Theseus	49
The Dead Tree	51
Dark Moon	52
From the Song of Inanna	53
Venus Retrograde	54
Now	56
Sanctuary	58
Mi Esposo Por Un Año	59
Theory of String	61
The Hole	62
Cord Cutting	63
Mend	64
Hungry Ghosts	65
Awareness, Heavy Sudden Rain	66
The Ell of Love is Loss	67
Doraemon	69
Daddy	70
The Male Dangerous	71
Gilgamesh	72
Returning Friendless from the Stars	73

Sketchy	75
Heretic	76
Tantra for Beginners	77
With Charly in Berlin	78
Husband for the Night	79
Aunty Betty	81
From the House of Africa	82
Tuvalu	83
Dreaming of Someone Like Liam	85
We Baked Well Together	86
The World is a Wheel	87
Fountains Abbey	91
Notes for the Day	92
Untitled	94
Acknowledgments	96
About the Author	97

Preface to the Second Edition

I brought *Love Songs for Boys* out in early 2021. I'd not expected to publish any poetry before the point of death, so this was either going to be one short year or the world had other plans.

During my 20s I was convinced that, like mastering tai chi or growing a forest, poetry took a lifetime. Minimum. My habit with poems had been to edit them to death until whatever spark within was very much out. It was not until I returned to the flow of painting in my 30s that I remembered how to write like a kid - how to let the play come through without thinking and when to stop and let go.

Miss Rona's pandemic swept across the world and I decided to look through a shelf of old journals. Among scribbles, sketches and volumes of pain there was the occasional poem – raw, reckless, and with the eyes of a painter not a critic, ready to fly. I collected them, typed them up, organised them into a body... and still hesitated.

As I sat around thinking about this collection other poems started coming through. They took a different form, translated from dreams and haphazardly typed into my phone at 3am. Almost a year on, I woke from one such dream to write it up when I realised this was part of a whole other collection and to bring that to light I needed to quit stalling and start rolling.

I'd had a work of non-fiction published a decade before, by O Books, but my experience of the world of poetry (and my place within it) suggested that if I wanted to see my writing in print I needed to make it happen myself. It was thanks to meeting Gay Afro-Puerto Rican poet, essayist and speaker David Nazario that I learned the possibilities of on-demand publishing and embraced the terrifying leap from one day never to now.

I brought *Love Songs for Boys* out in March 2021 and thanks to the loyalty of friends it made number 16 in the Amazon chart of LGBTQ poetry for about a minute. Thanks to Boien Hristov, whose experience with digital design, unlike mine, actually existed, the collection not only had a cover but a beautiful one at that.

I found the experience satisfying and inspiring. Almost immediately I played with the idea of bringing my queer fairy tale *Ghostipus* to light, knowing that for this to happen I would need to work out what Photoshop meant. I also knew that *Ghostipus* would need to be printed by a company specialising in picture books, and this necessitated setting up an independent publishing company. By the spring of 2022, when *The Book of Moons* became the second work after *Ghostipus* to be published by La Pus Press, I knew that, although only a year old, I wanted to go back and have *Love Songs for Boys* join them.

This second edition differs from the first in a few respects. There are differences to font and cover, format and layout. I've included a few additional poems and also added illustrations. I have been honoured with an original "poem in paragraph form" written specially for this edition by the glorious David Nazario, whose poetry soothes, stirs and dazzles and is a feast for ear, eye and heart. I figured that I'd also need to write some sort of explanation as to why this edition. Which is this.

It's reassuring, over a year on from its initial publication, to meet with the collection again and feel happy with the poems and what they have to say. That's not to say that some of them haven't been touched and on occasion moved, affected by the inclusion of the new kids. But each still deserves its place in this collection.

What's most pleasing though is to know that *Love Songs for Boys* is now part of La Pus Press, not haunting the doorstep outside the party like an uninvited ghost with a blurry barcode. It's a small difference, but worth it.

Keone
Wales
2022

David's Song

Will you answer the call of the calling? The sing of the singing? The ring of the ringing of the sound of the love songs for boys? Can you hear them as they gather together in individual and communal chorus? Did you see it written in the psalms to tell the story of the times when all of us would convene? Yes. The love songs still sing. Same as the birds still chirp with the rise of yesterday's tomorrow. We still fly high and come back down again, the way faeries do. Will you fly too? Then fall fearlessly into the arms of God and Goddess themself? When the love songs are sung we gather from far and wide to embrace the call. Reaching back to lineage, to belong. When the love songs are sung we remember new ways of living and being. The breathing becomes a beating and the drum is life. When the love songs are sung. And David's song? Can it swim and belong in oceans that can be both deep and shallow, harrowing and narrow, blessed and loving all the same? The answer is in a name, like Keone that welcomes us home. To homelands unknown, singing a warrior's song whenever they croon. Listen closely when the love songs are sung. And slung. We come. We cum. We come. When the love songs are sung. For those who are both. The sage and the smoke. For faceless face pics that still Boom Bang-a-Bang. For Hair and Holy. For Roots and Husbands of Agua. For Mermen and The Consolation of Trees. For Dancing With Oby in Castles in Time to Music Without Words. For Amusement and Hungry Ghosts. We know that

The World Is A Wheel and you will too. When you listen to the sound of the Love Songs For Boys.

David Nazario
Author of *Make Love Your Religion: How To Put Love First & Succeed at Doing What You Love* (2018) and *Poems Written in the Bathtub While Cumming Out* (2022) both published by SDJ Press.

So many wasted kisses
So much unwritten poetry

(from the Temple of the Melissae)

LOVE SONGS FOR BOYS

Have You Got a Face Pic?

Round these parts
gay is still a dirt
that sticks to the heart like a dart
shot at from birth

Keep your head down and your profile blank

Don't stare too much
in the supermarket or public lavs
where
in tiny lines between tiles
desperate calls for love
pencil the cracks

Boom Bang-a-Bang

I didn't fancy you

You were another test to be sat
in that year of them

Your hair was straw
receding in the doorway of another suburb
same colour as the duvet cover
on which I planked while you hammered me raw

And I clenched against the pain by reading
the labels on the video cassettes of past
Eurovision Song Contests you'd recorded

Three minute pop

It was quick at least
Quicker than the two buses I'd taken
to get there

And I felt nothing after
but the christening pain
endured
like cross-country running to the lake and back
every other week

for the result of filing
into Mrs Walker's double maths on Monday
and saying I'd passed

Hair

Hair you know just keeps on growing
on and on
like moulding dough
sprouting the colander heads of childhood dummies

At first it's a game
One stray babe navigating the vent of an armpit
A first paranoia of odour
fanned into the only locker room topic

We gas it in musk and borrow a blade

but next day there are more
then legions
marching from arm to groin
sharing their seed with each eruption
spreading like lotion
running amuck up belly and spattering the chin

Coming as spore
as stamen
quick as the pulse at a couple necking in the bush
by the saturated litter of glassy pornography

Pruning just helps it shoot further

Looking ahead there are beasts
matted with goosegrass
sticklebricking their backs to any bed

Tongues along toes
and orgies of thickening thread
rimming the ear

In time even the smoothest are touched

A crone beyond bleeding
screaming through ungardened meadows in glee
releases the wiry truth from beneath her lower lip

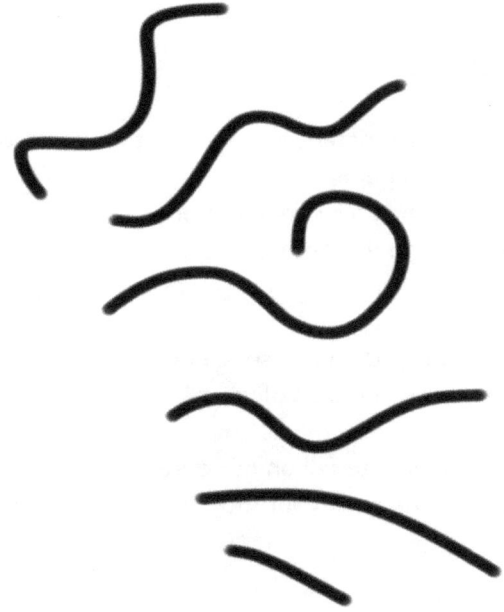

Holy

I bury myself in them
This pair

Don't even know who they come from
except the crucial rumour
that they once kicked a ball as part of a team

My nose explores changing room ammonia
tiles
northern sweat
some faint archaic legend of soap

and all of it works

Scent captures moment more whole than a camera
and here I am again
last on a bench in a room full of boys
who understand the rules

There you sit
when you sprayed your essence like epiphany
and caught me in the all of you

When I promised to fall on my knees
and worship the print your foot made
forever

Under Armour

In the bath
the duplex window shows us back

The man too big to fit
The boy beneath who hasn't grown

Lying beside you
bringing you close
how the years fall away when you bite your lip

till we're back on the sand
lapping lollies
damp and salty
with a clumsy hunger for touch

At the sauna once
a bull who'd built a castle out of muscle

Above the gym-racked fortress
that same face
defenceless
against the charging ball

The Rec

One man stretches and takes off his top
before jogging the perimeter

On a tump with trees
two boys
like bookends on a bench
sit smoking

By the basketball court there is beef

Boys in groups
wanting to fight
or needing

It makes as little sense now as it did then
when I hid from it
in someone else's garden

How
even while one of them is shaking
walking away
the other keeps calling him back
for more

like a lover

Atlantis

First it was the smell
crawling out from under the stairs
like a pond congratulated by too many leaves

That night I dreamt of bladder wrack
synced to the soundtrack of an advert for gin

Then the fridge began to sound like a duck
chewing nervously on its nails

The latest calamity is a low that won't shift
much to the chagrin of the board of CEOs
which hasn't yet
one suspects
reckoned on a tax rate for cloudburst

I feel how tired the roof must get
always covering for us

The cooker knows it's out of its element
Two frogs have kicked in
milk-eyed and patient
and taken up residence on the pedal bin

I lie in the bath and watch the last
welts of paint drop from the ceiling

The soap is lost
yet on the upside I can now float to the sofa

I hear puddles bubbling the phone
but can't decide which emergency to call

Needless to say the cat is far from happy
She gives me that look from on high that says
we tried
trapped between the Artex and a passing aspidistra

For the Ancestors

My flat has possibly eaten your grandmother's ring

I tut
feel nearly guilty on its behalf
like the parent of a child
who scribbles a masterpiece on the back of your sofa
but don't pretend to understand

Maybe it lives off light
gobbling diamonds

We turned furniture upside down
but only the dust glittered

Nothing was here

Except
how much more alive your grandmother
as we searched in her name

That old chair for the ancestors must have known

as if it saw
months later
your ring returning
where it could never have been

Waiting for you outside the front door
on the third step down

Swallows at Patmos

Where they come from or go no one knows
but here they are as free
looping round the villa
as boomerangs

Parentheses
exceptional
making sorties to the swimming pool
small thieves
come to steal back what they can
what they need

They flit over the filtered tub of chlorine
like exotic glyphs from a language
that translates freedom
either side of a rubble wall

Their pale bellies are shot like taffeta
Fleeting black-set jewels that skim the surface
and make sleight work of crime

All around they dart
from kitchen to cleaning cupboard
crisscrossing each other
and the men surely feeding a trunk of hose
into the water tank

By fig trees with leaves as open as palms
offering any whistling hand their pluck
of just ripe fruit

Flamenco

It is hot and I am lost
beneath this pinhole sin of sun
and unpardoning shade

Shoe follows shoe
over road slow-ditching curiosity
to ruin

I have fled as far as I could and still you determine me
In value, weight and distance
you are every measure

Through a louvered haze
kids on wheels stretch their throats
to banners of canned drinks and crocodile clouds
mosquito the wards of unfinished buildings
ministered by thin sciatic cranes

Without the hope of you
we are a saw-cut floor of toothpicks and tissues
wailing
for you
the castrated Madonna
for tornados of rain to kiss back the desert
with tears, sparks and a bullring of heels

To be in your arms
nothing but blood

In Halls

Your room takes me back

Bin spilling
Smoke noticeable
Ideas ripped off everywhere
and remixed on the wall

Single bed
No milk

We kiss
unspooling to music
as the sun idles across another day

I hold you and your hair smells young

When we turn off the light
there is no ceiling
just an Africa of sky
with its constellations of nursery stars
surely dimming

The Emptied

The day after you finished it
I went to your room where the window was open
wide enough to squeeze through

Whatever I was looking for
among the books
your fiddle case
that enduring ghost of tobacco
wasn't there

I opened drawers
as though we might be jammed in them

Still

In your bedside table
nothing but a pair of tights
tan and too late

I lay down the last on your dormitory bed
and stared at the houseplant you knew how
impossibly
not to kill

Ghost Trees

You drew ghost trees for tissues on the windscreen

They never wilted
hanging through the smoke and steam
of glass that would never be clean
like unopened envelopes of hope

Clear
and square
and evergreen

The Once Bowl

The once bowl wore a clean break

It had become *them*
and the two rocked on the floor
at the shock of separation

Amid the blindness of night
you slept on
while I was awake
witness to a splinterless divorce

I padded over
picked them up in awe
at how something could strike hard wood so exactly
there wasn't even a rumour of dust

Brought them together
where they gave no answer
save a line that shivered at the neatness of its own lie

Boy

The
boy
on
the
train
with
his
left
sneaker
off
wears
no
shame
in
his
smile
about
the
pleasure
striping
his
multi-coloured
sock
that
waves
from
across
the
seats

Beautiful Stranger

After we left the club and got back to yours
you put Madonna on and stopped kissing
long enough to ask what she was saying

I pray for you with tears?

I pay for you with tears?

Distractions

The question remains
what to do when the cappuccino ends

The tightly-packed girl avoids it
taking sips from the clock
which she thinks no one sees

A boy in denim waits for two men to acknowledge him
and offers to shoulder his mother's shopping

One of the men catches himself on the stairs
like the rip of cloth in zip
then vanishes through a gauze of smoke

This other woman
so indifferent she has to fake a double take
walks twenty yards in both directions

There are those with a tremulous fear of waste
who scatter past like marbles
but mostly they form a sedate, patient passage

The last swig is flat and bitter
and still the question remains

The Hunt

Never before or since
did sex come so long

did you have me riding through the night
mindless of time
as though we were back in the fairground
feeling your candy stallion pole
rise and dip
as the world blurred
and my eyes saw nothing through the sweat
but your high smile
dreamy
determined
from the bed through the lounge to the cooker

did my body release its singular quest to have
and instead be
ocean
boundless
bliss in waves unowned like wild fields

like the quilt that rippled back into place
after the morning you left a trail
for me to hound
groundlessly

There You Go

Meet your face
Tongue your mouth
Bite your neck
Push your head
Twist your nips
Sniff your pits
Taste your feet
Mount your chest
Pull your ears
Stop your breath
Gag your lips
Tie your wrists
Choke your throat
Spread your legs
Eat your ring
Tease your tip
Tug your cock
Suck your balls
Spank your arse
Smell your meat
Bend your knees
Hear your moans
Watch your spurts
Share your seed
Lick your sweat
Stroke your cheeks
Kiss your brow
Feel you shake
Hold you close
Breathe you in

Feral

I wanted wild and you obliged

Your piss tasted sour as old swamp
and you growled at the couple
looking for spare seats in the café
on our first date

You ate your food and grievances hungry
above a floor plaited with cat hair
and when you raged at your flatmate
you took out the bin bag and tipped it all over his bed

But you were the only one who noticed
my pits smelt of fenugreek
and when we kissed
every scent of unwashed laundry
stirred the cauldron of desire
we brewed together

When we escaped the city
the world made sense to you

The freedom to shit where you liked
with your smile
wide as the horizon
and an oyster of precum ribboning your dick

Shelling

There's the question
why do it
whispering your lips as I sit
with a fist of purses in my lap

We're so used to the economy of frozen bags
like shot bulleting the pan
that this seems archaic

I call you over and show
the definite *pop*
like a cue at the strike of a clean break

the huddle of each hip
released from the grin of sheath
like children from school

offer up the down of a spent pouch
so you can smell the recipe
of seed and mud and sudden rain

remember how the movement of fingers
in the pursuit of food
might feel like the unbuttoning of love
not battery

Husband of Water

We met at the beach
You pulling pints and me catching waves

I liked the run of your calves
and when you flowed after me and we kissed
it was the most Hollywood night of my life

You were pirate and skipper
boatswain and diviner
But for someone who healed every night in the bath
you never cried

Strong man
Leviathan
Washing machine lifter

You did anything but

Fell off tower blocks
sailed round islands
froze to ice
rather than risk dissolve

Until that day in December
six years after we met
Six years weathering my spotting
tapping and drumming

When you dreamt of the baby you
dead in the park behind your childhood

that dam crumbled from the flood
tsunamic

Did I ever tell you enough
how beautiful you looked that morning
when you couldn't stop weeping

How brave

Pearl diver of impossible waters
surfacing alive
red-eyed and liquid
reclaimed

Mermen

They belong to a stream of being more with fin
                      than foot
vesseled like tea in cupped palms
                                        spilling secrets
leaking a laugh at the rippling scene
                  they weave through in waves
                                        as they dance

In tears they take up arms
cast their nets with a marriage of muscle
                                and delicate fingers
save their breath to manage the slippery gossip
                of thread
        Brother tongues meeting like eels
knowing a cave

                                                Years
anchored in the pool of another's eyes
                        tracing like sand bars the lines
of a lover's hand

Caresses are promises hooked from a siren's lullabies
                  these men
the dreams dolphins make of land

Desire reminds them of a home between air and earth

In their hearts
        a mother's kitchen
                neither sunk nor burnt

In the Pool

In the pool at twilight
a lone crane stands sentinel
its crest a fan tickling the sky

Opposite
a snake shivers its scales
and insinuates its way over stone
like a rumour sharing an almost truth

For one breath the sun despairs
repairs below the silhouette of hills
as the moon ascends to her silver stage
full

At the time of neither night nor day
pooling the water
two fish go their way
each fascinated by the other's tail
for ever

Green Man

Come out the burning midday eye
into these dappled avenues and swim
in a green world of lazy leaf where
bird whirr and cricket tick
the changing radio frequencies
of numberless flies dissolve
like honey dew
in a jumble of fractured prisms
that catch the carouseling ash heads
above threads of new born spiders
learning to web across grass

And when you open again your eyes to difference
you'll find me everywhere

Roots

Is it big
Is it bare

This chair
isn't any longer a chair
by which I mean
sitting isn't happening

The feather-tailed weeds have moved in
and squatted the seat

Three central spindles from the back are broken

Even the ply-board sign advertising
butterfly chair
has flitted
littering its leaves like a book
no one reads

Only the word
chair
is clear
as a lie

The Consolation of Trees

I come to the woods to be long

There is no word for this
but the green of blood moss
on the rugged arm of the oak I sit in
and the canopy above
translates it

The earth here is clay
and the wind in the leaves takes me home
to the ocean

Every so often
a man I smile or nod at
but never see again
will pass and root me back
in a body that one day must join its cousins
in the endless possibilities of soil

Dancing with Oby

In the dance
orbiting closer
no thought but the body moving unto its own

Your smell
woody
reminiscent of a cabin somewhere mountainous
Cedar and sandals and high rocks
Your torso, sweat-varnished and sprung so tight
it seems ready to erupt

We curl into each other
sweet as honeysuckle round our trunks
until it has us
A part of the same tree

You know I dreamt about you
the week before we met
and the night after
explaining how you wouldn't call
because this time I was to walk on alone

Years later
seeing you at Dalston Junction with your husband
you said
we must meet again

and I think inexplicably of frogspawn
wobbling on the lip of a loch
waiting for its moment to leap

Scorching the Gorse

If I had time for poetry I might compare this
to an old Roman priest swinging their censer
dousing the gorse with gas

But farmers weren't paid to talk

They say it's prettiest now
though the thorns always flower
throwing a yellow coat as far as the coast

That's art for you
isn't it
always getting in the way

What matters most is keeping the match keen enough
to kiss the scent of petrol

Even on a windless day this elbow of land blows

Her mother first
then her
crying as she left
not at the char of grass
but how
for all my maps
I never got the measure

Never saw the fishing buoys as oranges in endless jelly
or the sea to be a milky jade
like the vase on that postcard she sent from Tibet

But if I had the words I would tell her
how the flames today looked like fingers
waving goodbye with hankies of smoke

I'd tell of a man who clambered the blowhole
of Dinas Mawr
bounded to the edge and over
legs pedalling as he fell
risking breath and severance and all the pain
a hard flexed arm of peninsula can summon

If I only knew where to write
to tell her of the gladness
as he tricked the last nick of rock
finding a bit of give in sea
the colour of a milky jade vase

climbing back to greet the spike
of a young uncindered shoot
amid the ash
that brushed at his ear

Samurai

Empty dawn park as it blossoms with light
I wait on a bench and unclench every finger
Vapour trails zip up the innocent sky
With clouds that do nothing but linger

First time remember behind the estate
Under a hedge so as no one would guess
Loamy ground rubbing our nerves and our knees
Gasping the air with our kiss

Always you'd call smelling new as fresh washing
Bringing in beer with a tinker of play
Slashing the peaches that fruited your cheeks
Smiling away the decay

Came here because you went made for a park
Dreamt of New York when all summer's rust
Your head in my lap watching sycamores skydive
Everything racing to dust

I knew what waited for you to return
That wallet-sized portrait of her and the tots
Tracing their smiles with all this pride
Nails dug my palms so you'd stop

Green and this hell built on words like *never*
I took down my sword to give you my heart
Green coiled my waist and twisted my arm
Slice and the night fell apart

Your head in my lap as I sat on our bench
Your head in the prayer of my hands at both ears
Roads to the airport, seat with a window
Whiskey dreams salted with tears

Green and this park is too wealthy with life
Ordinary pairs hand in hand with so much
My haveless hands waver palm up, palm down
Down and awaiting their touch

Castle in Time

She was a fire-headed four year-old
wanting a sandcastle

So we grew one

Excavating stone gems and worn jewels of glass
Dribbling a liquid beach
that baked itself hard in an instant

Turrets took shape as spire, as spiral
and with a need to safety it
she seized a redundant bucket and ran to the water
shovelling it back like a fury
to keep her fragile art from drowning

The castle rose
buckled
twisted
towered
until it ruled the bank of sand like an outpost
from a rag book of fairies and conjurers

Half-remembered shells frescoed its walls
A frieze of unicorn horns lanced the sky
and through meek holes amber light leaked
from the reminder of a beer bottle

She giggled for its finish
Hugged her toys at the gateway of adventure
Got close enough to catch perfection's moment

when the tide drew back
threw all its might upon the shore and there
before a blink could complete itself
rubbled it all

Nothing remained
but a slate of grit in ready empty innocence

The very essence of loss wretched out from her wail

Her face
a mangle of savage betrayal
like a mask from a city before brick
couldn't yet know the churn of life
blending all that was and would be

missed the sufficiency
the reassurance of a noisy beach
which hadn't noticed a thing
but might one day remember that castle
in time

an insight to our most mother shifting in her seat
cradling both rise and fall apiece
watching us learn again from scratch how to walk
with disappointment itching at one of our two feet

Ironing

When I was young I never reckoned
why my mother set asked a time each week
to work through piles of laundry

Life's too short for setting clothing straighter
surely

Now I gather with each corner
such a need to make amends
Those rucked relations that might almost be restored
by heavy constant smoothing
so removing every snag of crease and rupture

The guilt of wrinkled brows
persuaded to become again undamaged flat
Steaming over conversations that weren't had
went bad
with ends that never closed as neat
as steady weighted effort on a seam

We make certain to press on

So even if the promise fades
like heat does once the plug's been pulled
here's your clearance
for the week at least
resolved like the bed you'll lie in later
made up
of course
immaculate

Music Without Words

You send me music without words
and where it takes me is somewhere
like how the land feels
at the shifting lip of sea
or how the air trembles along the stave
of old telephone wires
just as the birds are fledged

Major Arcana

The Fool

You have to step into the unknown
for all that the mountains are orcas
waiting

The Magician

I see crows
in flocks and alone
They wear your eyes

The Lovers

In another time we were dolphin
friends
lovers
twinning the blue invisible

The Empress

Only reality edits
and her wings are closed
like safe scissors

The Tower

You brought the house down
It fell away like a cut of ice calving
with one feather-weight kiss

The Hanged Man

Inevitable is spelt
with the claws of a cat
who won't let this one go

Death

I took my name on the witch's land
chambered my burial in a cave
and dreamt of one more life where we
couldn't be

The Chariot

They brought me to you smashed
carried me back
through curtains of aurora
and home

The Hierophant

I tell myself
it was never that you weren't meant
to be broken

Fortitude

Only that we have more strength
than we fear
and time enough to discover

Roses

After he came
after we kissed again goodbye
and swapped names
mine
his
his partner elsewhere
I saw the synthetic rose on the gravel
and placed it at the cup of a rowan's diverging trunk

Miles from here
the other rose
the living one you gave me
must be dead as paper

He tasted of salted caramel
It hurt at first
but nothing like it did
getting on a road
that drove only away from you

The Nun Fish

The old woman whose house I'm cleaning
sat up in bed and shared a tale of a friend
who'd fallen in love only once when
on the eve of her wedding
her betrothed announced
he had to leave
to become a monk

I cannot see the friend
except to know how her mouth must have gaped

A sudden nun   howling
Her map to the future
binned by an instant fist
to litter   hitting her
like a fish on a slab in a dry world
where nothing swims

In gothic tales
this happens on her wedding day
and she never leaves her dress
until lace despairs to web and its cream
sours to butter

The message to her niece
(the one you saw mirrored in your night)
to catch another fish
hook them with a line
rip up their gills
and leave them

round mouth shocked

I get it
When she said her friend saw no other door
but the one leading to her own seclusion
because here too there is no path
that doesn't lead away from you

White walls
Small daily jobs
Cleaning dust off old books and glossy sills

Breathing the same stupid *Oh* for the glass

Single Bed

If I hadn't realised when I first saw the room
I knew as soon as I brought my shrunken life
through the door
and sat in its melamine emptiness
on the single bed

There had been a man
years before
standing patient
alone
in a peach suit
before his dwelling

He titled his head

The magpie on the chimney stack opposite
turns to face the western setting sun

The traffic from the city is far away and sounds
brush
brush
like the sea sweeping

Amusement

In the glass box reflection
a boy offers up his hand
to be met by its shadow

A coin slot

Amid the mass of cuddly faces
the three-pronged grabber closes
clings
swings back with nothing

Alcyone

Matter embarrassed you
weighed you
restrained you

You were butterfly light
heart-stopping as a rainbow
and just as out of reach

We met on the internet
(where else?
Your natural element
a form that could never be touched)

Kissed in dreams
Eyes closed
Continents apart
Sending emojis across the planet
One sun rising as the other set

Till I had to know what you felt like
and swung across oceans
easy as a trapeze act
believing you'd catch

I came back to earth at the cottage
near the creek in the woods
that you saw in your endless mind
and cried to the distant winter of stars
your sisters

After Theseus

You don't even need to wave a boat goodbye

Alongside
your cats pad
and in the glass of most feared
your self raging is also sobbing

Both of which you can hold

Look around the white crystal beach
on which you've been stranded
The cliffs are singing in bloom

Far above
Pele roars down the night
and below
shelters glow with the flicker of folk
just moving on

Listen
Simply
He wasn't ready for you
You weren't ready for him
Get back into the spin
until you fall and are found

Both of which you can hold

Across the water
Old Bones knits all

She is weathered wise
and fasts the cloth to your marrying hands saying

Husband
Bride

Both of which you can hold

The Dead Tree

Is a frozen moment
stripped of green
and sapless

Is for now standing
though the story of swelling
has left it

We see the sighs through which the light will pour

Its exterior is a stolen treasure in a museum
worn smooth
by nameless millennia of touch and crack

Next to it
a moorhen creaks

Within
some billion tiny tidiers
and more
eat it to dust

For now it stands

Another rush begins its splinter home
to a playground for children
and lovers to remember by

Dark Moon

Midnight
by the hollow ponds

Rain

Sheltered by an oak
two boys
cloud-lit and hooded

Together
Wordless

Waiting for the wall of water
to break

From the Song of Inanna

The horn
the boat of heaven
is full of eagerness
like the young moon

I baked for the wild bull
I baked for the shepherd Dumuzi
Perfumed my sides with ointment

The shepherd Dumuzi
filled my lap with cream and milk

He smoothed my black boat with cream
He quickened my narrow boat with milk

Venus Retrograde

This then is lust
which it has taken me all these years to name

How it meets you at the door and before words
your mouths have melted

There was a dressing gown
a harness
fishnets

Now there is a bed
a beard
tight spirals of scruff

Eyes the colour of that chocolate
with too much sugar
you know you must avoid

There is the way a freshly showered body
ripens with that brand of sweat
that ruins your knees

How you fit together effortless
The impossible cock that is both
more than a handful
and slides down like ice cream
off a hot tongue

His hole ripples like a curtain
in the breeze of your breath

The taste of his bum on your face
on your fingers
leaving with you

As you walk away
the one thing you know
though it causes your goddess of silk and oil to howl
is how you must shut the door
and never go back

Now

Now is not the time to think of you
or anyone else
unless with love
and the deep gratitude
that right this minute
no other person is in this room
interrupting my water

Now is the time to moon bathe
with these crystals hanging at the window
on a sky that has suddenly cleared

Now is the time to breathe in
the silver blue night
and dream

Sanctuary

We take our sacred spaces where we can
making them from nothing more
than a toilet cubicle

Out of the foot-fallen streets
and waves of river traffic
off the pier head of conversation
away from the froth and snarl of coffee machines
the endless mobility of button thumbs
with their promised potency
too slick for meaning

Far from this we sit
retreated through door upon door
until the cube that holds us

A coffin of toilet roll and shelter
Silence all the more satisfying for trinkets of water
shimmering down distant pipes
while the rest unknots to nothing but breath

Wind channels smooth through a patient vent
and here
prayer to a passage
beyond even that

Mi Esposo por un Año

So Photos decided to open to the June
when we began

That most picture of you
at a book signing in the sky blue shirt
caught unawares like light
engrossed

For weeks we spoke
and I didn't even think you were gay
just one of those luminous straight men
able to talk about love
and cry

We marked off every month
with a moon that was always full
and the world was ours to date

You folded yourself
out of that forest green Lada in Havana
and into my arms

At Teotihuacan
you conquered the sun by camera phone
while I met with the moon alone

Every moon until our twelfth
when our single sun
set

Amongst the mess of ending
I choose to remember a heart circle
where we stopped hurting
long enough to hear the other sob

How we held hands and prayed
above the Thames

Singing along to Proud Mary
for Evelyn
Hive Tina
and all who burn
on the turning of the river

The Theory of String

There was a ball of it
Wool I took to wrap the gifts
I'd brought for you

I didn't think it was anything special
until I snagged it
threaded through the belt straps of your pants
holding them up

when
in the magic of your fingers
it became precious

Part of you
Part of me attached to you

I only realised how we join us when
later that day of separating
I cleared the table
and found those coils of candy string
you'd wrapped my own gifts with

How could these little twisting threads
go anywhere else
but with me
wherever I move
as I pull on the rope back to you

The Hole

Setting up the shrine
the incense stick slipped and burnt the cloth

It is no longer brand new
marked now
by the haphazard accident of life

When we spoke earlier I noticed how
the hem of these shorts had snagged
and a trickle of pink thread ran down my thigh

Sometimes it's a sigh
or tracking where an eye goes

The first scuff on a trainer tip
A rip at the seam of a wrap

The tap, tap, tap of wax
as it crumbles the smooth column
of a pillar candle

Cord Cutting

In the end it was simple

Last time you were here you said
that pendant had a different thread

And now it does

Now it is on the thread of the invisibles
that links all and nourishes
without setting off the alarm

The other
poor dead old thing
that kept us cuffed to suffering
beholden to cold dependency
was as ready to break as we were

All the candle had to do was snuff it

Mend

There's this old seam that flaps on
It quivers in the rush of any passing wind
paddling with an eager tongue

There has been mending
but this part has stayed unmatched
like a door on its latch

The next is less true than the last
the rooms offered
smaller

Other wounds are sealed
Hungers sated
Gapes
up shut

This then must be repair

Picking up the dropped thread
working it through the eye of a bone
and carrying off the scars

Hungry Ghosts

Through the jungle of the belly come the horde
who clamour for more and narrow-eyed weigh
the deceitful insufficiency of plates

They thrill at the ringing jingle of tills
tug like children dizzy on Dib-Dabs
fizzing for every flavour next

Streaming box sets by the shipping crate
Wheeling luggage loads of chocolate
Licking chicken by the bucket

As Pac Man gobbles tablets in a maze
they eat everything
but appetite

A million intestinal minions
call me on
surging with urgency

and all they are saying
behind a heartbreak of greed
is

Hold me
Please
Let me know you'll never leave

Awareness, Heavy Sudden Rain

Repair water damage
There
Those deep orange pools you turn to after feeding
Water

Remember you belong
are never alone
Even as you walk
love smiles gently
and opens her wings

There is a thread which surrounds and imparts

Sleep well
Be

This is a vast family and you are just one of its children
Vital
Unique
Minute

Your mother watches over you
and all the roots and branches

Know you are alive among it
Like a trail of elephants
your family
sky walking and on the street outside

Even the clay cow with one leg missing is included

The Ell of Love is Loss

Why is the measure of love loss?

I can't remember when I first heard it worded
but my body learned at seven
after the volcano of my parents' marriage
when the new was a scorched earth of hissing
and third degree burns

I cupboarded my nerves to ask my mother
if I could still visit Aunty
And although she wouldn't speak to her
my mother agreed to drive me to a Little Chef
midway between Swansea and Cardiff on the old road
to drop me off

I was a drug deal
wordlessly handed over either side of the weekend
between two parties who needed to work together
but didn't trust the other
as far as they could shank them

What I remember
crossing the narrow chasm from my stoic mother
wet-eyed and betrayed
outside her white Austin Allegro
to Aunty and Uncle
jiggling near their blue Hillman Avenger
was not just guilt
not just excitement
but the unavoidable trade-off between the two

How it seemed impossible to move through the world
and reach happiness without causing grief

How inextricable the link in my step
between gift and desertion

Doraemon

He was a small thing really
A pin-head sitting on a table of importants
fixing it all in place

This Japanese cat that once jangled off an outmoded
phone found on a flagstone by Swansea Central

When I gave him to you
you barely noticed
but in his speck lay the spark
of all the parts of me
I'd raced to give away

Cuddly Mr Men
Dinosaurs and all that Rubbish
Holy Stones with dragons on

My heart's breaks
pooling in the music you never played
and all those unanswered doodles

The tears no one else but me was meant to catch

When I unearthed a patch of him last week
it was like a blue sky reminder
to press this next to my chest

and keep it this time
somehow
close

Daddy

We never stop looking for the gone
especially when they haunt us through the still

Like the familiar stranger in Benjy's 2000
from Palestine
who came back with me

And later
as we kissed
rolling over and under each other like a Celtic knot
there you were

Daddy

I swear
back from the dead and alive in him

I felt you in his eyes, his arms
the thicket of pubic hair
and the pulse of blood
through his thickening stump

Mostly it is less a stamp than a whisper

In the bald patch of the guy turning away
The volume of the one who won't call back

I look out the window each time they leave
and replay the sight of a street
packed with absence

The Male Dangerous

Is you
in that man over there

Is you
watching, assessing
weighing his balls in the scales of your hand

He is the knife on the kitchen counter
the mirror that once was hanging in the hall
but will for always make a jigsaw of pieces
that splintered away from your skull

He is the gambolling lamb leaping for your neck
the spittle milky at the corner of his mouth
as he inveigles you into the confidence of his threat

How he lightly jogs up to your bloodied flight
to escort you back as though to a dance

He is the rock bouncing in the palm like a ball
before it is dashed
The blade drawn on the diagonal with a whetstone
like a mower's meditation
The deadened calm
with which he kneels on your throat
as you would to deflate a spare mattress

Listen to how his silence thickens
darkening the sky
before he

Gilgamesh

Backwards he walks
slow
penitent
bowed

removes his sword from the wound
wide at the side of the shocked forest goddess
whose eyes and mouth
had circled and now at his receding
smile

welcomes every log of timber down
from vault and ceiling
folds away the forts to seed and acorn
plants their dreams upon the waiting naked verges
and dappled lit-through greenways

All his tablets known by hand
erase their scribbled tallying of pay
summon again the call for cat and queen
while
post by post
those heart sick seem again to find their path
to laugh and play

forget defence
embrace the ready land

Returning Friendless from the Stars

He did what they dreamed of
Plucked a guitar and launched himself from the gutter
on a one-way ticket to the big time

Endless space expanded to his voice
and older stars became spotlights
orbiting the singularity of his pants

Every girl on every street
knew his favourite make of drink
and no man had a name for the cord in their chest
that loosened at the comet of his smile

Global
he circled continents
lassoing deals that left him owned
by everyone but himself

until his size became
first joke
then curse
and the cameras yawned
at every clichéd chord change of his mouth

No one noticed when he left the leisure club of angels
crossing galaxies for answer from physics
mystics
shaking his gold like a beggar at anyone who passed

He found the mother of a child the aliens did borrow
Stood for days in the desert
praying to the sphinx of a nameless nebula
to be allowed his return

Sketchy

A man is a sketch
something dashed off
unfinished
the simplest lines as straight and blocked
as Minecraft land

He is the tail
knocked off the lower limb of the X
losing a little something vital
from mothers eternal
all the while trying to clamber it back

with towers, steeples, banks
religions, prophets, tanks
surgeries, weight-lifts, wanks

Always missing a little further
the very part he can't stomach to lose

He steamrollers hedgerows to seize it

If only he could mind himself without it
he might take the sketch and celebrate
its almost status
moving past battle
with that adorable wobble
accepting his less as her lesson for him

then finding the very part that most escapes him

Heretic

We are
the moonlit stranger
your child points at

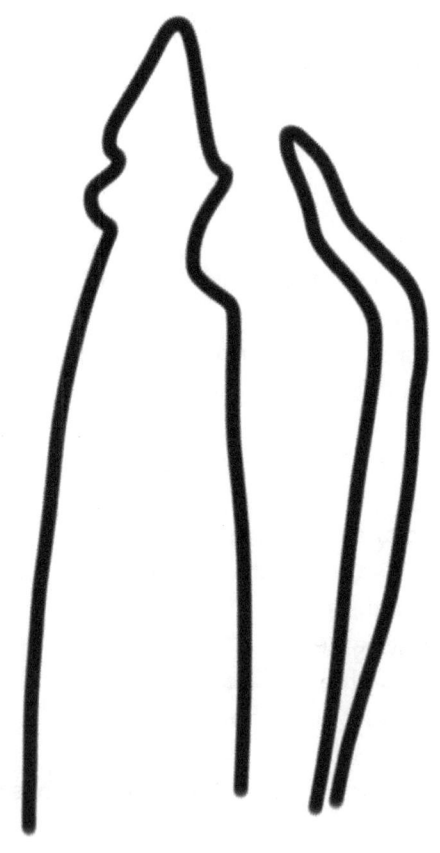

Tantra for Beginners

On the doorstep all
shoes were grey or mud or black
except the pink pair

With Charly in Berlin

How you concertinaed your legs
and lay down to sleep on the bench
under the willow just budding
on the banks of the Spree
by the last surviving stretch of wall
painted for peace

like a child
waiting to be held
who could never be told enough
how much love there is

Husband for the Night

You were here for the weekend
Traveling

See the world
you said
for as long as you could

I took you to a hidden garden
You photographed bees on phlox
and the spirals the bench ends cast in summer

That night we chatted in the pool at the bathhouse
Under a thunder of railway lines
our skins sweated fresh on the exercise mat
in the bricked cubicle
with its indigo light

We found somewhere to eat and you shared
the ventilator that kept you from dying in your sleep
the sight that was daily leaving your eyes
where you were traveling next
while you could still see

We walked nowhere in particular
ate ice cream arranged like petals in a cone
and ended up kissing by the railings
of a locked London square

We knew we'd never see each other again
and for the first time I got why the ancestors talked

of being married for the night

How miles from there
I can still trace the curve of your lips
your cock
the ghost of your fingers wedded in mine
for the length of an ice cream bouquet
never meant to be anything but gone

Aunty Betty

I dropped my lunch on the book the way Aunty Betty
used to on the Daily Mail she'd post to us
after finishing it
from across the street

Aunty Betty
who wore the same nylon jacket smeared and stained
from the same menu of meals
that punctuated the daily stock of horror like
MY DRUGS HELL!

Aunty Betty
whose house I never entered but on whose doorstep
I'd wait for Tupperware to offer or be collected

Aunty Betty
who had floors but not really carpets to speak of
and a kitchen like in TV shows about the war
Who stuttered over certain words and whose laugh
was like visiting a cemetery

It was said she'd been knocked off her bike
or fell
There had been an accident
Always that moment where it tips from normal
and breaks

Hoarding papers and boarding windows
Spoon not quite meeting mouth
Marmalade all down Mrs T's royal blue evening gown

From the House of Africa

Go back far enough and we are all there

We are a moment of lightning on the horizon
The priestesses in white
chanting and dancing

That naked witch child flying on the back
of a mythic cat

We are forest
and those pathfinders through it
River and velvet crocodile

Goddess Moon
rising from the volcano
amid the stone mosaic
of a barber's floor

Tuvalu

Where you go now Tuvalu
If not to somewhere out of view
Where skim stone tail
Of wave back whale
Be sunk like sunset in its spume

We dreaming reach you Tuvalu
Recall the time your breath we knew
And sleep with flowers
Whose nectar showers
All scales and trunks and lips with dew

You can be leave us Tuvalu
As how the green of tree times do
Through winter eyes
Those barren cries
Make stinging ocean heaven blue

Go rise again from far remove
An ever resurrection prove
Both shoot and pod
Each seed and bud
Do teach of how round time renew

One day we sail you Tuvalu
On plaited flax leaves dry with glue
The fish shall cheer
And land done fear
To feel the step of human too

Until then rest you Tuvalu
Curl up your woods, your rivers too
Keep sure your wings
Like feathered hymns
To times harmonious once and soon

Dreaming of Someone Like Liam

We're on the replacement bus service to the south
stuck in traffic
stretched out on two seats like we might sleep

Instead we look at exposed brick in a shop
and agree it's pretty

It cost you whole hundreds to get here
and how do we manage now

Maybe I'll get a job in Chicago or Dacca
and see you there

On a video
Adore Delano is dancing in bleached denim

At one point you go for a walk and I wait in a room
where people pray with their heads on cushioned seats
and a bright girl in a scarf teaches about the Prophet

You come back from the market with the Tao of Pooh
wrapped in a wedding train of paper

We decide to go on by foot
because really this bus is going nowhere

We Baked Well Together

In my heart I see us meeting together again
always
at Glastonbury

On a field with an incline
green and buzzing

You're building some insane set
out of plants and macramé and stardust
and just the sight of you
shining and neon-tipped
like when we were rolling together
and span around

I am currently chopping vegetables for soup
remembering the time
you were so purely and exactly you
and I was lucky enough to witness

That sketch you made from nothing
Those galaxies you took me to after the bong hit
feet to faces
The way you didn't hesitate to catch me
when I pretended to faint

And some of it broke us
And some of us we broke
And all of you I love

The World is a Wheel

From here
the world is a wheel

Feet walking across the sky
Shoals of clouds that streak in herringbone scars
Head on the ground
The field encircled by trees in midsummer dress

It is a wheel
as round as the mouth of a drum
or the always O of a song

We are here
Freewheeling
The still boys
The drones
Droning on

Elsewhere
other men have let their Queens
pluck out their cocks and put out their lights
taking back their seed for the next

We are the ones who haven't
or have and been spat out
or will maybe one day and not stop that hope

Those who've already decided to return to the woods
and make a home in a hole

We
the still boy drones
are humoured by the hive
but will be pushed out in time
to die honey drunk
amid the grass

The world is a wheel
and already we are spinning somewhere else

Already that vision has passed into memory
and even the repeating of it
feels like labouring on a part
for a machine that is no longer needed

We are the dancers and cartwheelers
The fanners and fire spinners
Doodle-dreaming fools and honey monsters

The bikes faint on the floor
Their wheels drift in space
with nowhere exactly to go

as the sun walks her way down the steps
adjusting her hem
and the clouds darken to a dirty blue

The world is a wheel
There is nowhere now to go
and yet everyone is getting in their cars again
to get there faster

There will be weeks
when people walk through the set of their old life
pressing at the scenery to see what gives

No one is sure which way is up
or where exactly in the park we are

but the dogs want to dance
They bound up as far as their leads allow
and lie belly down to maraca their tails

We eat honey
and already there is something royally different
at work in the jars
The runniness is thickened and envenomed

We eat in vast sums
as though we suspect we might not know when the
next meal is coming

The future has not been planted
and right this second
we are pulling down the past with ropes
and tipping it into the dock to be judged
like a witch

We begin to imagine a world
that might better sit in a museum
A museum of the stealers
instead of the stolen
A museum to sugar

We can't edit our history
you're right
so we must compost it all
Smelt the bronze back and pour it into the mould
of a cat

When we dance it is like we are knitting ribbons
to a May Pole
Over and under and over and under
remembering the weft of it

Death is now a daily feed

Across the field
another circle of boys kicks a ball so high
it will land with a thud

The world is a ball as well as a wheel

One toddler extends his arms and flies towards it
while another comes up
to show the butterfly hennaing his hand

A two year-old has the dance in her large dark eyes
as she tambourines her beaker

They know

Fountains Abbey

Most of the walls have gone from here

In its persistence
the chapel looks like an architect's embellishment
not so much desecrated as half asleep
contemplated
a work in progress

waiting for the couriers
and scaffolders and theme park managers
to return in hooded order through the visitor centre
bringing back each a piece of honeyed boulder

How nature sings on though the psalms are lost

That strange haze
where a breath of breeze ushers chords
from the distant chancel of leaves
and a waterfall

And if none come to build again
the grass will only flourish
at the arch of limestone blocks
that lapse a little more each day
to the touch

Notes for the Day

Wake up
Remember to come back
fully
Stir

Smell the day
Thank it and your back
in postures that make hieroglyphs of the body

Stop
Breathe
Feel the dewy grass

Move slowly the rippling energy
in a lazy steady dance

Drink
Cleanse
Fuel
Play with the cat

Write in colour
Teach a little
mostly how to fly and dream and hear

Read the tales of others
How they wandered away from the point
until they returned without knowing
to kiss it

Doze
Feel the multitudes of soil
between fingers
Sow

Stitch the worn together
anew

Swim in the hammock
between the lines
where water licks coral sand
and an always endless sky

Think well of the world
and all the smiles peopling it
even when you are sad among them

Love
as far and wide as you can reach
for nothing else is real

Be kind
to yourself first

before
sleep
gently
summons you home

Untitled

You ask
what is true love
and as far as I've the word for breath I would say

true love is nothing out of reach
but stands by a bus that waits for you to say goodbye
and lets you on without taking
all the loose change you can pan
that fails to make a fare

while familiar adolescence
wide-eyed on the hilarity of crossing a road
wrestles its way through irrepressible bodies

where a festivity of stars casts its frost-spotted web
like a mirror-ball
above the discotheque of sky

recalling the hands a friend had just held
promising to listen
for as long as they've ears

and to give in the purse
some near stranger forgot to remember
she'd dropped
to the driver

as you reach the end of a small day's lifetime
in the arms of someone who kisses you home
for all that you snore

Acknowledgments

Thanks to: Alcyone, Alex, Amy, Andy, Ange, Antonio, Bo, Boien, Chadia, Charly, David N, David T, Elizabeth, Ely, Emma, Erica, Francisco, George, Giles, Imelda, James, Jane, Javier, Jayden, Jon, Kyros, Liam, Libby, Lil, Livia, Lou, Margaret, Matthew, MohJay, Nathan, Nia, Nico, Noah, Oby, Paul, Philip, Quinton, Rhidian, Robbie, Ruth, Sadhu, Samir, Seb, Simon, Sophie, Tim, Victor, Will, Yaniah. These poems wouldn't exist without you.

About the Author

Keone was born in Swansea. Their poetry and articles have been published in a range of newspapers, magazines and pamphlets, in print and online. *Hereafter* won the performance award at the inaugural Pint-Sized Plays competition (2008). *The Parable of His-Story* was published by O-books (2011) and translated into Korean (2013). Their paintings have been exhibited internationally and are in private collections around the world. In 2016 they coordinated *Sacred Art*, an international contemporary group show in Aberglasney, Carmarthenshire. They set up La Pus Press, which has published queer fairy-tale *Ghostipus* (2021), a collection of dreamings *The Book of Moons* (2022) and *Love Songs for Boys* (2022). They are always Wales, even when they're away.

www.ingramcontent.com/pod-product-compliance
Lightning Source LLC
Chambersburg PA
CBHW030306100526
44590CB00012B/544